# OVER THE ROLLERS

Joe

A souvenir.
I've really enjoyed
working with you.
Stephen

November '04

By the same author:

*Rumours of Cousins* (Yorick Books, 1983)

# OVER THE ROLLERS

Stephen Plaice

Canterbury

YORICK BOOKS

1992

*First published by Yorick Books*
*at 27 Manwood Avenue*
*St Stephen's*
*Canterbury*
*Kent CT2 7AH*

© *Stephen Plaice 1992*

*ISBN 0 947710 12 4*

*Printed by BPCC Wheatons Ltd*
*Hennock Road, Marsh Barton*
*Exeter EX2 8RP*

*For my father and mother*
*Allan and Joyce Plaice*

## ACKNOWLEDGEMENTS

Some of these poems previously appeared in the *London Magazine, Poetry Nottingham, Poems for Peace, P.E.N. Anthology I* and *Cumberland Poetry Review.*

# CONTENTS

'What is rumoured does not vanish, if many
rumour it, it becomes a kind of goddess.'
Hesiod, *Works and Days*

# OVER THE ROLLERS

There are parties on the lower river tonight,
the winking lights of houseboats under the willows,
the soft glow of cabin-cruisers permanently arrived.
Music and laughter caress the waterline,
someone is shouting 'Surprise!' but it is more like
something we have all known for a very long time.
Among the mature purples the moon stands aside,
the hostess turns as if to welcome it on board,
but there is no smile, just a leer of bilious disgust
as she casts her olive-stone accurately into the dark.

We are not going to that party,
nor to the others that flare along the banks.
There is something in us that wants to feel
the sudden snatch of cruel fingers above,
the tug of the sunken devil in the mud.
Up around Deadman's Bend, they say,
the pole slips into delicious nothingness,
and the water tastes of champagne as you drown.
We will own the places where we make love,
moaning there like fallen soldiers,
thirsting as the night wheels on.

In the morning, the crunch of clean gravel,
the lucid Sunday bells tumbling in the sky,
breakfast in the watermeadows upstream.
We will keep this dream of morning.
It will survive wherever I hurt you,
even when you are far away and buried
in the business of other people's lives.
It will come to you especially at night
and uninvited to my endless river-parties
with the moon and the young whispering:

'Tonight, tonight,
tonight we're going over the rollers.'

2

# PHOTOSYNTHESIS

When photography began, the world stopped.
The pony and trap held patiently still.
The farmer's wife in the doorway turned to stone.
The labourer with shouldered pitchfork
stiffened into his respectful pose ten paces
from the awkward earl enacting his daily stroll.
Only the unruly tree continued to swirl,
filtering the pale summer sunlight,
spoiling the edge of the treated plates.

When our ancestors began to picture themselves,
they wished to preserve their stationary world,
even though this is also the very moment
from which we have measured its decline.
The labourers went quietly into the factories,
land values rose, the farm was sold, resold,
the track became a lane, the lane a road
which still bore the farmer's family name,
but a hundred families came to call home.

Slowly the pictures too began to move
and to occupy us for whole hours of the day.
Now we sit and watch a moving world,
see more than we could imagine alone
or ever experience for ourselves.
We observe the acts of love and death so often
—even follow the salmon journey of the sperm
and the transmigration of our astral souls—
they no longer move us to pleasure or to tears.

But sometimes when the images pall
and we step out, no further than the gate,
for a breath of the half-refreshing air,

3

stand motionless among the cars,
surveying the life of our suburban road,
it feels like we too are being observed
by something much more ingenious—
and there is the tree still absorbing light,
the oldest camera in the world.

# IN DOCKLAND

Where the ships came in, dream me alive.
I wore a veil of estuary fog
and a hempen rope of hair.
A whistle could blow the veil aside,
a pull on the rope raise my skirts,
let the negroes and the lascars inside.
They gave me their tongues and their oils.
They were my cocoa and my tea.
One night the fog was ether,
it felt as if I took the crew on board.
You were my only child.  You cost me.
I pushed you out into the world
cradled in an orange-crate—your first ship.
You were molasses, sweet child.
Did they refine you in the big house
and try to make you white?

I've looked for you often since,
along the wharves where the fog
used to curl around the woodpile.
It is permanent Sunday there,
all the captains have gone inland
to find a new religion.
They have invented the overhead lines.
As long as we go on I don't mind.
Your children are my children,
bring them to visit me sometimes,
and do not think badly when you scent
my delirious ghost solicit
the gaunt warehouses now.
Don't dream the purity that was.
Whistle.  Dream me alive.
You are the blend that I began.

# THE GHOSTS OF THE VICTORIANS

For her they were all in the future.
'Who is that gentleman in the morning room
tinkering with the tip-tap machine?'
Elly often frowned over one eye
and said things like this unnaturally
when they were quiet upstairs
and I had time for my needles.
'Isn't that the tube, Elly?' I said and she went.
But then it quickened.
'Nineteen-eighty-five, six, who'll live here then?
The Nabob of Krishnapur and his seven wives,
the Admiral of Her Majesty's balloons,
the inventor of the speaking lines ...
It won't be no Davenports for sure,
their breath is as short as a thimble.'
'Elly,' I said, 'that's no way to talk in service.'
She was church-quiet, but then the frown came again.
'Who is that lady in the morning room
squinting at the click-clack machine?'
'Mrs Fanshawe,' I whispered in the pantry,
'that girl will be in Cold Harbour
before the sloes are ripe.'
But it was the Fever took her.
The Doctor closed the frowning eye,
wiped his hands and said, 'From that incestuous clan
of monkeys out at Storrington.
Too many dark nights and daughters.'
He was a clever man the Doctor,
his linctus took away my cough,
but did nothing for Elly or Davenports alike.

I saw her once afterwards,
the day the youngest Master died,

6

she still had that frown over one eye—
'Elly,' I said, 'does it hurt you still?'
She pointed upstairs. The tube whistled.
I went. He was dead. She was right.
Since then the charabanc, the aeroplane,
telephone, electric light,
Mrs Fanshawe could no longer manage the stairs.
Now the mistress is dead. The Doctor is dead.
Old Mr Davenport has a bell beside his bed.
The tube whistles sometimes in the middle of the night.
The children, bless them, still love a game.
For me they are all in the past.
I remember over my needles how Elly once said—
'Nobody really lives here any more,
we are already safe, at home, on the farm.'
I like to think of us there, all of us,
not here any more, not in this house
I will be the last to forget.

# THE HOUSE FROM THE RIVER

Rounding the bend, excitement ahead,
children mewing at the water's edge.
It must be a Sunday in summer.
Families descending in ranks to the river,
sprawled on the lawns in the sunshine.

But drawing level, a sense of panic
spreading along the crowded bank.
Lost in the rushes a child crying,
the wail of a siren splitting the sky,
people splashing towards the boats.

Up there at the house,
stillness and solid shadows,
pink stucco absorbing the sunset,
forty windows oblivious to the scene.
The great great ancestors are taking tea.

Then a glimpse of the exceptional child
gazing out through the nursery bars.
It is not the scramble that he sees,
but swans on the easy, purling river,
his future castling in the clouds.

# THE BREWERY

At primary school because I had *brains*
Mr Savage sat me by the sash-window
that looked out on the brewery.

Its walls fumed sweetly all morning,
black engines muscled in to catch
the barrels wobbling down the ramps.

The midday siren always beat the bell,
brought the workers out into the goalmouths
to take the chances missed in the match.

Summers came, the wasps, the chimney's shadow
grew long, seemed to pace the afternoon,
hold off the moment of escape. I ran.

But those rowdies who sat below his desk,
and under threat of the rounders-bat,
stayed in until the yards clocked off.

Saturday I went that way to the match,
and from the engine-grooves picked bottle-tops
that printed a corona in my soft palm—

the brand of industry I'd later miss.
But now each time I ease off the cap,
the first whiff of that beer takes me back

to those *good footballers* kept behind
to make up for lack of brains by learning
silence or the art of brewing perhaps.

# THE LAST BARGE

The boy is still there
under the redundant mill.
All afternoon he has been watching
the impertinent minnows twitch the float,
its luminous yellow quill-tip deceive
the clasping dragonflies.
But still it does not cock,
begin its thrilling tipsy run ...

And then the grating of the gates,
the water flows back into the lock.
The last barge comes,
carrying hidden cargo under tarpaulins,
an old fox crumpled on the tiller,
and the fox-faced girl,
caught in mid-clamber, staring back
from beneath her coaly thatch.

Too late to follow.
Wait for the chiming laughter,
the sunlit daughters in their first bikinis.
Wait for the pleasure boats.

# ON LEAVING A PROVINCIAL TOWN

The rear-lights dwindling uphill
into the layered shadow-smoke
stretch out his idea of departure
across a steeplechase of fields,

as the Sunday bells which now begin
tell their traditional version of the evening
in which a sense of village is repealed,
except this is the edge of town,

a town already melted into photographs,
its pavements warming and cooling
through wars and snowfalls and carnivals,
a thousand years, let's say—of history

into which he was suddenly spliced
and yet has no business but to belong,
watching the flashing inter-cities,
the aeroplanes in the hems of sunset.

He's never left, has long since outgrown
the gang smoking under the chestnut tree,
and suffers at dusk the same farsickness
that once made hometown boys into soldiers.

Already he dreams himself, the local hero returning,
in the eyes of that beauty who turned him down,
the friend of everyone in both bars, a worthy
of these celebration bells, back for good.

Such boys turn into men one summer evening,
walking out slowly in the sun with prams,
like amateurs still in the Cup Third Round,
condemned to wish for nothing but luck.

# LAST CAFÉ IN THE WEST

In that town you've always passed through
thinking 'What a place to wind up in'—
one day you'll have to stop and try the café,
if only to put its melancholy to the test.

The steamed-up windows warn it's a trap
where the tea's been stewing all summer
and the special menu's left scrubbed blank.
You break the crust on the sugarbowl—

the jukebox fuzzes a Glitter hit,
there's just the waitress playing the fruit-machine
even though she knows it's fixed—
she'll talk to you because you smell of the city.

She wants to get away from here and act,
to leave the local champion practising out back,
she doesn't want to be his girl any more
and turn into the woman in the upstairs flat.

You'd take her too if the last chapter of Angels
didn't burst in, snap the chairs to beating bats
and leave the walls bleeding ketchup,
the waitress love-bitten and her tears unpaid.

You won't defend her—she'll wait for the next,
or take a chance on the soldier from the camp,
after too many vodkas at the dinner-dance,
and get pregnant down a lane in the van.

She only stayed here this long to play a cameo
in the dream you've been filming along this road.
Next time you come looking for the location:
clear glass, antiques, the woman in the upstairs flat,

still in a nightdress, her hair in a mess,
shouting down: *it closed up some summers back*,
as the red lens of the sun pans out on you—
last customer of the last café in the West.

# PIRATES

We've managed to steal a long weekend
at the rented lodge above the bay.
Nothing to do but comb the beach,
watch the tides replenish the rockpools
and the clouds sliding down the Lizard.

The first day, two dogs came down the track,
ownerless, uncollared, the leader
with a black patch over one eye.
They swarmed over us for treats,
left by the cliff-path as if whistled.

Returning next morning as magpies,
a typecast omen, breaking from the rocks,
one with something silver in its beak
scavenged from the rubbish-dump
last summer's tenants left out back.

Something is happening to the children,
they are wearing silk scarves and mascara.
Everything is still in the offing for them,
that three-masted tub rounding the head,
that black flag spied through their telescope fists.

This afternoon a seal periscoped,
suddenly reversing the horizon on us.
It must be tonight they are coming,
their torches inflamed with my brandy.
I have loaded the last of the muskets.

But we are already packing the car
as their lugger heaves into the sunset,
running in on the evening tide,
faces screwed into squares of rigging,
purple and orange, callous as crabs.

I can see them picking over our debris,
cramming their mouths with the sweet and the savoury,
falling out over a forgotten earring.
Only their leader can utter more than oaths,
spinning his cutlass on the mahogany.

I can hear him at my little wheel
as we drive through long-subdued villages.
I can hear him through his accent, pasty-thick,
as we are swallowed back into the town:
'You hired us, you fuckers, now show yourselves!'

# WRECKERS

Those who stalked the crippled ships
along the cliffs—what would they spit
if they returned mob-handed to ransack
these half-slated inns in which the English drink,
only to find the flotsam of their own hovels
salvaged for the decoration of a myth?

To think the pilchard coves were looted for this,
a marinaded version of the monstrous sea retold
down boyhoods by old salts darning sharked nets,
warning of shivering crones, cave-dwelling freaks,
who warmed themselves on timbers torn from decks
in oil-skins ripped from the nearly dead.

Sea-widows who foresaw the end from the rocks,
keening like cormorants, their shawls windstretched,
ready to descend on every stitch of sail-cloth,
while those even the press-gang would reject
salted the dumb tubs in their hidey-holes,
too deep for the probing excisemen.

Thus the new harbour-masters portray the poor—
whose gutted cottages they now winter-let—
a scavenging pack waiting to strip the ship
of everything it has gained through fair trade,
hell-folk to raise the hairs on rubbernecks
who want their extra lashings of The Storm.

Relax.  This is where old hulks come to rest,
so best believe the lobster-pots and tacked-up nets,
ignore the bill still urging us to fight the French,
and let *The Revenge* out of the bottleneck,
get wrecked, and float west down past Land's End
to the limpid kingdom of Lyonesse ...

But back along the quay, by the holiday flats,
moonlit, we stop to raid the sunken skip
for anything the new people might have ditched,
wondering, as we retrieve a chair, not whose it was,
but whose gleam this is, stealing over us,
and how quickly we inherit the unfinished wish.

# STATIONS

### I

The last shriek of the whistle
seemed to come from inside me.
I cried non-stop to Coventry,
then only at the major stations south.
Euston was the terminus of summer.

Its soot-furred galleries
smoked in a century of steam.
The blackened stoker smiled down
from the infernal cabin.
'Would he like to see?'

I was lifted up in grubby hands,
introduced to the furnace,
that child-hole in the beast
which had brought me away.
Its fierce heat dried my cheeks.

We rattled back on the local,
stopping at every miserable halt.
Outside, the world beyond emotion,
tufted bricks and liquorice wires,
sunlight through the milky panes.

I was silent, picked sullenly
at the scars on the carriage-cloth.
'Don't worry, you'll see her again
—next year,' my mother said.
It might as well have been a lifetime.

She came one afternoon in black furs,
with her suitcase and another uncle.
It was all electric now, she told me,
but I had stopped crying openly by then,
child of an age of steam I had hardly known.

II
Victoria was the mother we had left
to join the legion of the unkempt.
We came back like beaten soldiers,
washed-out from the boat-train,
having failed to find a cause
worth fighting for or against.

Lost was a feeling we had to invent,
tramping the liberated roads
through poppy fields enriched by the dead.
We nearly all came back unharmed,
the children of a safe crusade,
ready to love our mother again.

She was unimpressed, a severe matriarch
who had seen her sons return before
with lumps of shrapnel in their backs,
sweetened with the morphine whiff of death.
We came back with briquets
and duty-free cigarettes.

Even now Victoria receives us with contempt.
Tippling breakfast sherry, agape,
the nut-brown dossers, her real derelicts,
risk their heads over the parapet,
shamble out of their lavatories
to watch us dashing for commuter trains.

III
Leaving Paddington on the Intercity,
flicking through the paper, ignoring London,
my head tightening with a midday hangover
full of other people's voices, bridges,
headlines, unfinished poems ...

a sudden flash of half-apprehended aims—
those thorough engineers in tailored coats
consulting their reliable pocket-watches
to ensure our future prosperity
arrived in Templemeads on time.

Stars, Castles, Counties, Manors, Granges, Kings—
my grandfather admired these engines,
butlered to the class that built them
so that his son might one day enter trade
and afford a proper education.

Their past seems full of such purpose,
of struggle through jungles, cities and exams,
only for us to leave its solid platforms
and breeze west on a broader gauge,
buckshee on the Great Western Railway.

At Swindon I closed the paper, took out my pen,
composed a memorandum for my grandchildren,
stranded in the future with their doubts—
'Do not be overawed by our achievements,
we only tried to build our weakness out.'

IV
I must have passed through Waterloo
the year we went on holiday to Weymouth,
and once or twice bought papers on the steps
when working as translator for the famous.
But I've imagined journeys from that station,
and that one day in a sunlit compartment I might
meet the daughter of an understanding patron
who would loan me a wing of his mansion
and an antique escritoire looking out
on endless gardens permanently in flower.

Today, she's there, behind *The Independent*,
but something stops me from leaning forward
to begin that watershed conversation.
The points have been changed up the line—
I'm side-tracked into a weed-choked siding
where the engine sits still coupled to its tender,
the Pullman with its faded SOUTHERN legend.
Inside: inkstand, silver pen and holder,
the etiquette waiting on the lamplit table:

*IF YOU HAVE ANY COMMENTS OR SUGGESTIONS*
*REGARDING YOUR JOURNEY ...*

beneath which in best copper-plate I write:
*'That stretch between Salisbury and the Junction,*
*the trees are too significant to waste as scenery—*
*instruct the driver to go slowly, stop more often.'*

# BLACK DOG

The black dog was everywhere in that ghostly county,
the weaver could not leave him at the church-door,
but carved him on the end of the family-pew.
And even when it was summer and the children unsewn,
and the weaver's son lay pinned to the flaxen girl
in the sun-burnished nave of the baled harvest,
the black dog brushed so close he felt the chill
and saw a reflection pass like a rain-cloud
through the cornflower blue of her eyes.

The weaver's son became the weaver,
the flaxen girl mother to four still-born,
and she took to speaking to no one but them.
The day the weaver caught her behind the barn
drowning the puppies in the stagnant pool,
he took to flailing her with his fists—
this being all that was left to them both.
She stood then silent, much outdoors,
staring at the sails turning in the vacant sky.

A frost-bitten fisherman returning over the broads
heard the singing of the maiden ice,
the ticking of the claws,
found her coffined in a transparent dyke,
candied red in the sunset light.
It was a wool burial, the gravedigger left room,
and alms were handed out amongst the poor.
In the ale-house the fisherman opened his bestiary,
and the drinkers walked home in fear of the Galleytrot.

By day the black dog lay down on the grave.
On relentless nights in his isolated hall,
in the flicker of the fire that did not warm,

23

the weaver watched his shadow dance on the panels,
saw his wall-eye gleam in the tankard's bloom,
and ascending the stair with his threatened candle,
heard the ticking of the claws on the flagstone floor.
By night the black dog lay down on the bed
and chilled his feet to clogs of ice.

For years the weaver fought him, fled him,
but the black dog was everywhere in that ghostly county.
One night when the sky held nothing but the flaxen moon,
he called him, fed him, caught him by the tail,
he spun him, wound him, threaded him
into a tapestry of cornflower blue
and sold him in Ipswich market-place.
And when his work prospered and money came,
the weaver married the Woman of Delft
who bore him four sons before she died.

So he raised a Perpendicular church to her memory
with a great nave-window so that the light might touch all.
But he still could not leave the black dog at the door,
till he paid a carver to carve him closer to God,
up in the chancel on the misericords.
And there he left the black dog.
And when he died, his four sons, the wool-merchants,
carried him to his church in a coffin of oak,
buried him in linen with the woman of Delft,
and alms were handed out amongst the poor.

# RENAISSANCE STEPS

Rising from the reeking shambles,
morning breezes plucking at my sleeves,
I rushed into the cool institutions,
taking the steps in twos and threes.

That was the hour of the new beards,
when talent jingled in its silver spurs,
all the doors above were open,
all the stars were wanderers.

Inside, benefactors pretended
they had worlds at their fingertips,
they twirled their globes hypnotically,
turned my ambitions into ships.

Now I sit among pagodas,
screened by forests of bamboo,
I watch the children's flying rockets
climb into the future blue.

Here the random winds becalmed me,
in the cockpit of my sedentary age,
the stars look through my telescope,
the steps dwindle to a narrow gauge.

The spirit ascends until it enters
the secret uterus of space,
it is reborn upon the idle plateaux
where the giant pandas pace.

# MELANCHOLIA

Girls, under this tree where you sit observed,
tittering, sipping your bright lemonade,
Melancholia sat, heavy with her third son,
as yet unnamed, but destined for the church
unless the first grew sickly and the second fell.
Of all the Earl's stately trees she preferred
this copper beech, a sport as yet unnamed,
sat there with open book, closed parasol,
on sunlit days when the leaves grow darker
and from a distance smoulder against the greens.
Above her the grey convoluted branches rose,
an allegory of the swollen roots below.

All through August and in her eighth month
the gardener brought her a daily offering
rolling in her flat trug—a single lemon,
the first the orangerie had grown.
She waited for his shadow to lengthen,
modestly, as one about to disrobe,
and then, though his gaze was still upon her,
she gnawed greedily at the zestful rind
so the juice ran, staining the pages.
With puckered lips and unfamiliar teeth,
she sucked long on the bitterness in the belief
this time she succoured her God-given girl.

It was late September when her waters broke,
she refused the doctor and his sweet phials—
'I will see no man but the gardener,'
she confided to her maid. The gardener came
bringing the last sharp fruit as if by design.
'The English summer does not suffice to sweeten him,'
he appeared to say, looming tall at her feet,

his beard seething with bees like a honeycomb.
Later the Earl came muddled with claret,
his veins etched as clear as the back of a leaf.
'Do not be angry with me,' she heard herself speak,
'I am carrying the gardener's child.'

A smell of camphor on the stairs.
The boy was delivered on the sopping sheet,
and God took his mother in exchange.
In the scullery the maid set him to her breast,
as she had done his brothers before.
The gardener crept back to peer through the crack,
with his eye upon her she felt at peace,
but fear at night with no one watching
as a crapulous hand fumbled at the latch
and rough whiskers scratched the nape of her neck.
October mornings staking out the sheets in the wind,
she saw Melancholia musing beneath the black tree.

The first grew sickly, the second fell,
the Earl's estate came down to the third,
thin as a winter reed, fox-faced, feminine,
more suited to the cloth, the village said.
In summer he browsed in the orangerie
with only marble Nausicaa to play ball—
the gardener long since back in the Downs.
In winter, as a man, he shared the sculptor's longing
for his homeland's more definite light,
with number and symbol, hermetic device,
he sought in the night the elixir of life,
but thirty English summers sufficed.

Girls, under the tree where you sit observed,
Melancholia sat with her pitcher of tears,
till the green-stained stone blended into the garden

and her meaning was lost on its inheritors.
They dragged her with chains then back to the house.
You may go to her now, that door is open,
or you may rest here under the gardener's gaze,
never wondering what brought you out in the light.
Even now that all is named and the lemon cheap,
from a distance, most girls seem to choose this tree,
till the shadows touch and beauty streaks.
Then they rise up and go inside.

# A NEW EMOTION

You are in the light before summer rain,
the pink light that transforms the streets
and makes the city ancient and empty.
Even when I'm walking there alone,
from the doorway of a popular bar
there is an expectant music playing
that tells me we are about to meet.

When the rain comes it is confidential,
a conversation with you tonight
even though you are not in the room.
It varnishes the sullen garden
and sweetens the crying of the swifts.
They spread the word through the streets
I am about to write.

That word must be more than love,
if love is a passion for the strange
or a fear of quitting the familiar.
What is it the quick swifts know?
They have been conspiring with the rain.
They slice the air like scimitars,
carving the huge signatures of change.

# THE BULL AMONG THE POPPIES

All that month a field of poppies
blazed along the road we took to work,
while opposite, in a triangular paddock,
a bull was fattening for the show.

I imagined I was in love.  Talking to her
could send a shudder through my bones,
and on the evenings she drove me home
I checked the fields like a proprietor.

That scarlet carpet, that alabaster repose,
were ciphers of something I wished to own
or ancient opposites to be resolved
in myself and in the world.

Halfway home, they broke our conversation
(her daughter's sleeplessness, my poems)—
I imagined her naked body
spread out in the fire glow.

At night, searching in a book,
her scent did not go cold—
Demeter had no husband, I read,
and saw her yellow hair unfurled.

Every day I felt the shudder deepen
and the atmosphere between us grow close,
it was hot and the bull lay down,
the poppies were full-blown.

The moment seemed to approach,
then stand still in the heat, deferred.
The next generation was in love,
we saw them coming through the corn.

July.  Mirages waved on the tarmac.
The storm the sky promised was withheld.
The field faded and the bull was shown.
The work became mundane, the road.

When she cleared her desk
she left me a typewriter.
It shuddered through a sheaf of poems.
They made the fire glow.

Until winter driving the road alone,
an image floated in across plain fields,
greater than memory, in suspended strength—
the bull among the poppies, cooling, content.

# THE RELUCTANT GODDESS

The girls are blazing into motor beauty,
the silk is taut across their breasts,
they pile their hair in golden castles,
worship themselves with cigarettes.

Their eyes are ringed like distant targets
to draw the darting glances of the men,
but only one girl has the power to make
trees blossom merely by embracing them.

Yakshi opens rounded as the water-lily,
resents her own voluptuousness,
wishing she were thin as rushes
unnoticed at the water's edge.

Yakshi smiles to please her lovers,
but freezes in the hollow of her flame,
they clamour round her in the darkness
are singed, compelled to come again.

Though she denies that she is chosen,
they garland her with effusive flowers,
strew her pillow with their paper-money
and stammer out their marriage vows.

Love women only for being women,
she hears profane philosophers advise,
at night she sees them creep with tapers
to light her statue, look into her eyes.

# THE ROMAN RETURNS

His laugh is a coarse intrusion
upon the breathless concubines
spreadeagled on their sumptuous cushions,
surprised amidst orgasmic chimes.

'You are fluttering among the doves,
have you forgotten Asclepius' cock?'
He returns the standard to their love.
They deftly spring the armour-lock.

The skirt is lifted, the helmet plucked,
they coo sarcastic over battle-sores,
one smooths in oil while the other's fucked,
'Why must men make such stupid wars?'

The question hangs upon the air,
they stop his answer with their lips,
Venus awards a triumph to the pair,
he can't beat their Babylonian tricks.

The eunuch brings the dripping taper round,
smoke cools through the waterpipes,
mosaics shimmer on a golden ground,
they dream the future archetypes.

The soldier with his sheath of flowers,
the woman with her stiff winter rods,
in dreams put on each other's powers,
self-sufficient as the gods.

No short sword, no stabbing upward thrust,
no conquest, jealousy, or fuss,
it is these dreams we pretend to trust
until the Roman returns in all of us.

If he wakes he'll want to know,
what devil taught them while he was away,
he'll drink and smash the painted bowl,
they'll call the lictors and make him pay.

Best then to leave him sleeping, slip out
to tease the boy who stokes the hypocaust,
he says there's a new tribe going about
whose love is genderless, unenforced.

# THE SERPENT

A woodpecker taps unseen in the stillness,
and suddenly we are no longer outside,
the creatures are biddable again,
the white mare slopes from the beech-wood
to feed from our grass-filled hands.
Unashamed, we watch the treading ducks,
the greedy carp sucking between the lilies,
the closing angle of the clasping dragonfly.

This is a place of lush pleasures,
but he has grown listless and tired
of what he knows, too urban and preoccupied
to look at the variations on a leaf,
the comma on the underwing of the butterfly.
He would like this world to be simplified,
believing the Garden is the certain youth
he has already begun to leave behind.

Some close as the Garden opens,
but she knows that the Book of Moses lies,
and that at the centre there is a single Tree
where life and its knowledge are entwined.
Though she has grown in silence,
pretending to defer to his mind,
she now leads him down the subtle paths
I sweep ahead of them in the dust.

I hang looped in the Tree, waiting
until she is naked again in the dappling shade.
The breeze hisses in the leaves as I unwind,
whispering before the closing of the gates:
'Eat more of this, eat more of everything.'
Soon her heavy white haunches will be wise,

and her unnamed daughters know the better lives
forbidden by the fallen god of man.

# THE MAN TO TRUST

At last it's just like the ads,
the dinner's eaten, the coffee's plunged.

She slips away through the partition.
A shy half-smile.  The moment has come.

I cradle the brandy-balloon.
Well-being spreads through the room.

Her books and posters approve
my reflection in dark mahogany.

Suddenly she's back, hair re-puffed,
placing herself gingerly in my hands.

It's slim, fresh to the touch—
she knows I'm the man to trust:

'Will you read this
and tell me what you think?'

# ON THE LAST DAY OF DECEMBER

The tree that fills the window
shows the structure of summer.

I feel my skeleton shift
gently in the flesh.

The sky is neutral,
the sea unimpressed.

Nothing in the offing,
no omen to be read.

I mark this passage
as the passage of rest.

Before the wind revives
the waves and sails—

Sends the New World
skimming into port—

And the first-footer
up the path, out of breath—

The man with the message
urgent on the knocker.

# FAREWELL, MY LATIN MASTER

That afternoon where the yellow light,
not sodium yet, glowed warm inside,
eyes down, scoring our boredom on the desks,
we leant, one elbow planted, one ear cocked
ready to receive the wisdom of the classics,
you gave us Juvenal, over bi-focals,
construed that passage with a halting catch,
the one you said no one forgets:
*Farewell. Remember me. When Rome returns you*
*eager for rest and peace to Aquinum, ask me*
*from Cumae to visit you, and your Ceres and your Diana.*
*Unless your satires are ashamed of me I'll stride*
*in heavy boots through your cool fields to hear them.*
A few of us stiffened, raised our heads
as if we suddenly scented clean air outside,
the satchel-tossing freedom of summer fields.

Indeed I am tired of London,
of friends bickering in half-paid houses,
bored with the partners they barely scratched,
sleeping in whatever bed seems warmest
and already dreaming of the next.
My dreams, no better, seduced by naked holograms
of the listless Swiss telephonists in my class
who sit considering their spectacular nails
while I am side-tracked to satirize my past.
But now sometimes, saying goodbye to them, I hear the catch,
fight the tears of which school first disabused me,
as Juvenal and your voice comes back:
*Farewell. Remember me. When Rome returns you ...*
But then I have to go and look it up.

39

Farewell, my Latin master, and rest assured,
a few of us have not forgotten this much,
though Rome, Berlin, the Pound have fallen,
but not yet the Bomb, at least on us.
In the white light, should you return one afternoon,
you will find us grown yellow and cantankerous,
in heavy boots, urging our flocks of Eurogeese along
to honk by rote the Past Continuous you called Imperfect
so that they might somehow pass the echo
of the echo of that midnight warning on.

# EARTHWORKS

Once more the fields prepare for war.
He walks the path between the wire,
complaining sweetly to the lyre
the bunker-scars the diggers claw.

The poet's vision's gone polaroid,
the war of words was fought in vain
we're so much radiation in the rain,
another layer of the coming void.

He scans the future countryside,
the spectrums out beyond the rainbow,
the ultra-violets in the hedgerow,
where the feral humans hide.

The larks scare from the tumuli,
he sings the spirit that will survive
but when misjudgement day arrives,
will his reactive lens tilt to see

the unborn and the dead descendent
from the gold-trimmed canopies of cloud
carrying lambs and sheep-crooks, loud
with anthems he should have written to defend them?

# THE LANDSCAPE

When I asked him why he had come,
he said, 'I have come to repaint the landscape.'
'I am rather fond of these old colours,' I said.
But he shook his head. 'Everything must be repainted.'
I watched him mix the new colours on his palette.
There was midnight black and fiery red.
'But they are such simple colours!'
'The simplest,' he said.
I watched him set up his easel.
It towered above us in the sky.
'How long will all this take?' I said.
'Seconds,' he said, 'split-seconds, less.'
And then his brush swept the horizon,
obscuring the outline of the hills.
The sky was midnight black,
the earth was fiery red.
He turned to me, his face as grey as lead.
'Why did you let me do that?' he said,
'You could have stopped me,
you saw the colours, black and red,
you stood and watched me mix them.'
'I am an ordinary man,' I said,
'I do not paint landscapes.'
'But it was your landscape,' he said,
'and now your sky is midnight black
and your earth is fiery red,
and our faces are grey, as grey as lead.'

# THE BATTLEFIELD
*Lewes 1264*

When the sea sucked back the Ouse,
and the mud was smooth again, they rose,
still in the saddle, unvanquished, erect.

The selective morning sunlight flashed
on pommels, helmets, tempered breasts,
webs of clinging mail smoked blue.

Low-tide. One spluttered into life and spoke
a stream of bubbles through his vizor,
then slumped as the mud relaxed.

Some of the proper feeling returned,
I prayed to the Lord and his pitiful saints
that all the king's men would collapse.

But the oblivious tide refilled them,
voices came to tell me that I might live,
that we would never see battle again.

Wounds heal. The Ouse meanders. The field forgets.
But sometimes a sword rings under the plough,
I feel the warheads buried in our river-bed.

# STORM 87

After the thrill of the standstill
we secretly wanted to last,
it's dubbed a freak of history,
a domestic dinosaur in the past.

Hasty books are published, pulped,
the storm becomes its photographs.
The newsclips recall the newsclips,
lovers re-chisel their epitaphs.

The weather's the only revolution
that levels all things in its path,
when even insurance men are equal,
gnashing in the aftermath.

We've ushered in the age of safety,
and moved to International Park,
but locking up last night I swear I heard
that hooligan whistling in the dark.

# CHRISTMAS CROWS

What mortal fear could be set against
the fullness of the children in the snow,
or future epidemic put at risk
their carefree treble carolling?
Their faces shine all day undimmed.

Even the accountant turns alchemist,
mixes a cocktail of Christmas fizz
to chase the faded golden sense
of gifts that were once his to give.
But pantomime statistics trouble him.

The innocents in the wood ripped to bits
or trampled by pale horses on the road,
the kids who get their final kicks
from a poisoned apple or the witch's kiss.
It is a time for cautioning.

High above, as he calls the children in,
a pair of circumspect executors sit
in professional black, sharpening their nibs,
waiting to indent in red reckoning ink
the necessary losses amongst the lambs.

# THE WICK

*'If illuminated solely by a flash of lightning, the*
*motion of all bodies on the earth's surface would, as*
*Dove has remarked, appear suspended.'*
John Tyndall *Death by Lightning* 1865

Summer printed on a winter page.
Morning sunshine on a Boxing Day.
Visitors open all four car doors.
Michael and I take his new football
down to the Wick where the frost
has melted to a sheen of dew.
Mud under grass.  We choose the driest patch,
by the tree, that infamous tree
stripped by a stab of summer lightning
that killed two sheltering boys last May.

Michael has already forgotten them.
He wants to be a goalkeeper,
to be tested with penalties, hard ones.
As I spot the ball up, he stands tense,
weighs which way to dive, or if to dive.
'It's a death or glory situation,'
as Peter Shilton says in *Shoot Annual* '85.

At my back, summer is waving in the heat,
families are spread out on chequered cloths,
swings, football, a sense of pre-war contentment.
But then the commentary goes fuzzy on the radio,
the hedges come closer, the acoustics change,
the mewing playground seems further off,
then thunder, the first big spots of rain
darkening the pastels, anointing foreheads.

Only these two, resplendent in mint kit,
a potential pair of United wingers,
veering away from the central game,
intercepted by the spreading dark,
as clear as badges sewn on baize.
Those who saw it happen say the sky
was rent like a curtain from the top.
Others say the Wick still holds the shock.

Visitors open all four car doors.
Rose twilight on a Boxing Day.
Morning printed on an evening page.
'Even where death strikes ... ' I write,
but through the veil of frost a flame,
Michael still holding the muddy ball aloft,
having made the diving save.

# UNDER THE VIADUCT

Under the viaduct the millstream ran slack,
the nettle and the dock grew rank.
In August the yellow lilies stank,
shading the leech and the stickleback.

No other temple air could hush us,
lure us so far beyond the lease
to watch our smoke rise to appease
the river-god stirring in the rushes.

That month the reedcutter came,
punted me under the chill of the arch.
I called up into its dripping dark
and heard my sister whisper my name.

The echo vaulted overhead,
ran away to join the river,
but the cutter relented, let me outlive her,
I became his boy instead.

Long since I ride the chattering train,
sparking above on frozen rails,
glimpsing as the inter-city wails,
that silent, god-forsaken hole again.

If I'd gone with her, think who I might be,
not the complaining, cold one of the twins,
but the generous lover of divers and dolphins,
the great mother octopus spread in the sea.

# THE INVISIBLE COLLEGE

After the meeting at the publishers,
before heading through the heat to the station,
I spent an hour drinking your beer in the Arms,
entertaining the idea you might still live here,
and half-drunk, among the tourists, found myself
in Jesus Lane again, the gates of your college open
where I stayed for weekends two decades back.
Down the long-walled drive it clicked inside
you had been watching me all day
through the unpatched crack we'd left.

And stepping onto that fresh-swept set,
the lawns dressed like perfect wickets,
there was suddenly no one else around but you,
or at least that unlived portion of your life
in those amber quads you loved best.
No voices, no willow thwack, just an inner snap
of you showing me the crack in the wall
where Dexter once hit a mighty six,
and a flash of my red-brick distaste
for all the privilege assembled at your back.

It could not save you from the weather,
and the rude fate dished out on the road,
no worse, perhaps, than what awaits most of us
further on, though our work is visible,
might even last, like Chrysippus said,
until the final glory of the cosmic fire
in which even the wisest soul must be cremated.
But in that light death seemed academic,
choosing Pardoe's peg and not the next
on which to hang its graduation gown.

Now, home at my desk, still here years on,
incubating your unfinished translation,
more often I enter the invisible college
the living join in lucid moments
with those who've gone ahead, find you
in your corner study, stumped for a phrase
to render the feeling we could not render then.
I'm not sure if this version's mine or yours—
no matter, the best we've come up with so far runs:
'the slow forgiveness of the dead'.

# FALLOW

That year he left me fallow
I had grown weary of myself
yielding to the plough and the harvester.
Nobody disturbed me for months.
My ditches swelled then froze.
Foxes came foraging over the snow
leaving me pocked as the moon.
It was a relief to be empty.

Spring blew in disappointed birds,
the tractors turned my track to mud,
a stallion crashed the one remaining gate.
I rose in weeds and patches then
but hardly showed the summer come
or felt the slither of the snake.
My pair of lovers came to plant their seed,
but found no cover and wound on.

I parched. I cracked. My ditches drained.
Those wavy afternoons of hot mirage
I dreamed of what might one day rise in me,
below, where I slope down to the stream,
an ample house with folded eaves,
a shallow pool where the girls might bathe
among shading trees, and in the trees nests,
and in the nests the birds of heaven.

Autumn. Rested. I waited for him—
that clumsy farmer with his farrow
come to churn me up again,
slop his crop into my rich grooves,
I missed his aimless broadcast corn,
his turnip-head and swede,

51

even the hay I rolled his daughters in.
But no one came till spring.

Then men who work but do not sing,
exhausting me with silage, kale and rape,
leaving no ditch in which to breathe.
I grow bitter without hedge and gate,
deeper and deeper hide the plan,
determined not to show this generation
the cool villa or the mosaic snake.
Till better grows in them, I wait.

# TO PYTHAGORAS IN THE RAINFOREST

All things change, but nothing is lost,
consoles the wisdom of Pythagoras.
The soul is monkey, orchid, cockatoo,
it passes with the lightest brush,
stirring whatever limb and leaf it must.

But it is harder now to believe
that nothing goes out of this world,
as the loggers bring the canopy down,
and whole layers of livings collapse.
Pythagoras—can the chameleon turn black?

And will our god rain gold upon us?
Will he heat the air to melt the ice-caps?
And will the rain that would have tapped
its secret rhythm on the great green drum
enrich us beyond our wildest dreams?

Recently we wake from the rainforest
crying like lemurs in the lurid dawn.
The axes are cutting deep in the sap,
coming closer to our inviolate patch.
Open your forms, Pythagoras—
                              we are ready to jump.